Peculiar Motion

poems by

Robin Kirk

Finishing Line Press
Georgetown, Kentucky

Peculiar Motion

For Frances and Ray

heat in motion

Copyright © 2016 by Robin Kirk
ISBN 978-1-944899-20-2 First Edition
All rights reserved under International and Pan-American Copyright Conventions. No part of this book may be reproduced in any manner whatsoever without written permission from the publisher, except in the case of brief quotations embodied in critical articles and reviews.

ACKNOWLEDGMENTS

For me, poetry is an immersion in the world and in people that is unlike other kinds of writing. I would never have had the courage to write or publish without the poets who continue to inspire me: Wisława Szymborska, Robert Hass, Mary Oliver, WS Merwin, Nazim Hikmet, Sherman Alexie, Seamus Heaney and many others. My parents – Frank, Judy and my other mother Beverly - gave me a love of all kinds of stories, and those stories saved my life.

Publisher: Leah Maines

Editor: Christen Kincaid

Cover Art: Jessica Mink from The Harvard College Observatory Astronomical Plate Collection

Author Photo: Jenny Warburg

Cover Design: Elizabeth Maines

Printed in the USA on acid-free paper.
Order online: www.finishinglinepress.com
   also available on amazon.com

Author inquiries and mail orders:
Finishing Line Press
P. O. Box 1626
Georgetown, Kentucky 40324
U. S. A.

Table of Contents

Carolina Parrot 1

Lee 3

Harvest 4

Ishi's Cup 6

Old Roger 8

Andalecio 9

Cold Harbor 10

Craters of the Moon 11

The Daily News 12

Abstentia 13

Habit 14

A twenty-minute poem 16

The Capitol Dome 17

Peculiar Motion 18

I had this dream 19

A Theory of Strings 21

Charles Bridge 22

May Day 23

Beacon 25

Orison to the Gods of Lake Michigan 26

The Dark Army 28

Thanks to whoever sawed the limbs 29

I ate my house 30

What Ceres heard 31

Carrick-a-Rede 33

Red Planet 34

I want to know 35

Like a wave 36

CAROLINA PARROT

When Audubon drew them (parrots
gorging on cockleburs), there was
peace in the Carolinas, a few years

before the war. Parrots leap from the
print, pop-eyed, iridescent. A quiet man's
inside joke, since parrots aren't

nice. Parrot: thief, pest, interloper,
corn-stealer. At least, that's what
farmers told us, what farmers say

in the mountains where we saw *loros*,
raucous as teens, descend on ripe stalks.
Their infamy is global.

Or this: she jabbers like a parrot. He
parrots words. "At least the wolf
leaves us something. The *loro*

picks us clean." This, though, is memory,
when "parrot" is not feather and hammering
heart, but that insubstantial thing, a thought

in a story or what I tell you
about the image of a parrot, the sad
story of this Carolina bird last

seen in 1904, in a Florida bog, an immense,
green depth where there were no paths.
Call this the parrot's end, or when

we left our *loros* behind, on the world's
other end. So many times, we've left
what we know. When memory strikes,

it is exuberant, loud as a parrot, sharp as its
livid gleam in this too-soft land, yellow and blue,
the quick, bloody bite of remembering.

LEE

Facing South, how predictable! Lee
sits a stone-white Traveler, patient
through the years. Greedy

I was that night, in his shadow,
and not at all willing to wait
atop our king-sized bed, and you.

Confederate generals had their day.
Now I have mine, again and again, ripe
as the oranges in our sack at City Point

where Grant, joyless, awaited final victory.
Raw luck and the payoff, perhaps
of a previous, blameless life? Historians

write of plans and visions, men
who lead men. Sated, I yet crave
another whole life of you.

HARVEST
for Frances

Unsown, this crop
flourishes in the
thick bamboo shade:

Olde English, Shoneys,
Red Stripe gum,
Night Train. Untended,

it is replenished.
We did not
ask for it!

My fingers grow
sticky and wet
from this weekly

harvest of pleasures.
Other's, of course.
It's a glimpse

of lives passing
so near our
bed. What souls

these, what quick
charge races their
veins? I imagine

it is not liquid
flame, but sparks,
bursts, the candent

blossoming of July
rockets. If I
lift a palm

would I catch
one? A tiny
ember, heat in

motion, a life
caught and held
between us two.

ISHI'S CUP

Pain is the fullest cup
at the elbow or in
easy reach. Always.
Joy is found, perhaps

within sight, often
hidden. Expect it not
ready made. Find it
with the cup at the ready.

In rags, Ishi walked his cup.
Thick soles bent the brown
grass. Imagine the sky,
a blue, blue eye.

Shorn and burnt, who
recognized him? No one
on the globe. The cup
was his only familiar.

An ocean of further hurt
was where he thought
to rest it. Yet in a pen,
he glimpsed new joy.

Was it not so? It is hard
to lay down to die. Hope
is not reason or logic,
but tough as the fingerpads

that draw the gut bow.
Ishi stepped from one life
into another, cup in hand.
Step, he thought,

step with the toes
steady, the cup
steady, looking
straight into your eyes.

OLD ROGER

Oil stain like a leopard spot,
pink lips ripe from combat.
Cobweb face to the crack
in the door. He smells us.

A mournful cry. Hear me! Who
will rise? Food! The window!
I want to slide my caked, blackened
nose between the warm sheets!

Between sleep and the awakening
stretches the cry. And another,
and another. He is relentless.
Old Roger! He smells love.

You rise. I rise. Bodies
not bodies, eyes not eyes. Into
the cat night we are like tourists
speaking no language, knowing no stars.

ANDALECIO

Last night, you sold the house again. It was your secret.
Everything went: furniture, plates, sheets, spoons. In an
apartment, I mourned. It's possible my tears were snores

slapping like stones across a lake of sleep. This dream, the one
where you sell our house, replaced the one where Rudolph's pursuer,
the Abominable Snowman, bears his terrifying teeth.

Other nights, waves hurl me to the breakwater, tickets are misplaced,
children are forgotten. Andalecio appears in your spot, wordless.
He settles in to sleep. I huddle naked to the edge, aghast.

As a child, I feared the unknown. What I fear now is the unmaking,
the smell of sealed boxes. At dawn, I hear the racing of our son's feet
on the way to the toilet. The house is not sold. It's what we made

where we stash hope. Like Christmas lights, hope
with empty frames and too-small skirts, ready for a
a fine holiday and to shine again against winter's chill.

COLD HARBOR

Grant would not relent. Across
the gentle pastures he marched
again and again and again.

He lost. The fallen stayed
at Cold Harbor, ignorant
of their ultimate victory.

Would that they had known!
It was the last defeat and,
for that, the cruelest.

The Butcher Grant, the drunk,
he was called. Who wouldn't drink
with so battered an army?

Once again pasture, once again
a living place, only the mud trenches
show how desperate was the hour.

Who has not lost, and lost heart?
Victory is a silent traveler,
veiled to the sharpest eye.

In the closeness of the pines,
nothing is clear. There are
angles and densities, turns

that the mind takes, without
warning. Yet who can say
that victory does not creep close

in their slim shadows, by the
dogwood blossoms, as a breath
soft as January rain.

CRATERS OF THE MOON

Grace is not natural, but learned,
or so I thought as I watched the arm
go up and down, up and down,
in the rapt command of Juan's eyes
as they compelled it to move.

Motion is deliberate. Challenge
fills a baby's eye, not just delight.
We fall. We may not get up. The stroke
made Juan's bed broad as the moon
and as treacherous. Its white craters

and sudden peaks pull him down.
Beneath the moon's light, I think,
"I've made it this far." I feel every
cell, my dwindling telomeres,
thirsting for more. "What did I do,

in another life, that merits such joy?"
The answer, I fear, is nothing. I hang
like an astronaut, breathing prepared
air, hoping that the tank, the leash, my
shiny suit hold against the crystal

space that embraces us even in sleep.
We've made this. It's also luck, the
patient stitch, and our own minds
that bind us to a path that arcs
a fire of intentional fortune.

THE DAILY NEWS

Coffee, milk, cereal, juice
Night doings, infamy

Spills, a cry, the clatter of spoons
Earth's unstable crust, fire

A radio hums, laundered clothes
Hate and its twin, despair

The clock, the clock, when
is there time to read it all?

Toys splinter underfoot
Bones resurface, shoes

In the morning freshness
Another bullet finds its mark

Washed faces, scraped teeth
Breadless she sits

Its our world
The world is ours

Embracing small bodies
Delicate as kites, windborne

We comfort, clean, provide
Within our grasp, lives

They are all near us
The fortunate are few

These walls hold
Worlds in motion

Small, wet, new
Shelter against a storm

ABSTENTIA

Abstentia is the condition, a state, a habit
of saying no amidst plenty. Say, forgoing
that cake so moist and pretty, that whipped
cream, that hot slice. You could have it.

But you don't.

Which creates, of course, the absence of what
you could have had. That pleasure. Next time, you
reason, it's what you deserve. Instead of no, you say
yes and yes and yes. Until you are sated.

But you are never sated.

Be thin (and have that dollop). Be agile (but relax).
Work hard (but don't be pushy). Have that slice.
Be young, by the way, and beautiful and kind.
Get ahead, but create witty, personalized décor.

Just do it (or not).

Extremes would be easier. To gorge or
abstain, to lie down or run, to grow old and wrinkled
or fight each line with knives and potions. What
is written on the bone and skin can be erased.

For a time.

To abstain from you, then devour, is my choice.
I am never done. I gorge and forgo, reek of you
and watch. I eat the moist cake and covet, in public
or alone, reach for the hot, whipped, creamy slice.

You are my secret vice.

HABIT

"When passion turns to habit"—the phrase
caught my eye, caught in newsprint,
fit to print on Valentine's Day.

All cheap chocolate and sentiment and
the cool detachment of our sleeker,
sportier "new classics" way.

It didn't register until later, as I sipped
the coffee I sip at about that hour, reading
(at the more-or-less usual time) pages

C-1 through C-12. I thought: What
does that mean? The drudge of days,
unwashed dishes, car trips

where no one says a word. Is that
a kind of death? Once, the thought
of that black sheet left me dizzy.

A skid into the utter end of days.
Not the stuff of chatty columns.
It's only fair because it happens to us all.

I thought next of you, and your habit
of light caresses, walking heavy, trying
the door before taking out the keys.

The boy's hunger in you makes you
fill your cheeks, always anxious
for the next bite. So what's next?

I worked and walked and wrote
a poem for you, as I've done every
Valentine's Day. Habit pins hours,

moments fragile as frost. Without it, what is there? Talk, heat. Faces swept in the raw speed of falling.

A TWENTY-MINUTE POEM

Necessity brings me to this:
a meditation, squeezed into a day
of phone calls, tasks, the clock,

dropping off and picking up, and lunches.
It's an exercise in light, not the one beaming
6:43 onto my face, but the stellar beams

that link our days. To render light: how often
have you seen it probe her eyes, so fresh,
so like yours? A fast creek, water over stone,

fish backs green and rose and grey.
If you could, when would you stop time?
Where? Would you stand in the light

or just outside or get a bay-wide view?
You sleep, heavy with fatigue.
It's 6:51, by the blue light.

THE CAPITOL DOME

Two months after the attack, I walked across Capitol Hill and saw the dome lit from within. The hundreds of panes of glass glowed against the blue black sky of evening, more brilliant than the early stars. The dome itself looked like sugar spun into a fantastic shape, as if a chef had made it to crown a gala dinner. The sight did not please me. The dome appeared fragile, as if it could be brushed away by a careless hand. I had never thought of the dome that way before. Before, the dome had seemed a sturdy thing. A hum of voices revealed that debate was underway in the red velvet and marble and wood chambers. I could not make out what was said. It did not matter. I feared for the people inside. I feared for the dome itself, as breakable, it seemed, as a living thing. Even marble, with its veins and discolorations, can pulse with life. At the Galeria Borghese, Apollo reaches for Daphne as her fingers sprout laurel. I gazed at it once with you and could almost feel the warmth of the god's hip, so like yours, and the pressure of his arm as he touched the girl. The figures moved me not for what they were, stone and art, but for what they said to me, the sculptor's passion whispered like a secret across the centuries. I thought of that god when I touched your hip that night. It was as I imagined, as if the sculptor had seen your body and worked from it, making you immortal. I thought the dome, like many things, was permanent and indestructible. But in the cold of that November, I saw the dome delicate as laurel, as your hip, as words whispered in the night. Among the evening walkers, I willed the dome into my memory, I made it a part of my life, impossible to destroy. This I will not forget, I say, this I will whisper into your ear with the lines of this poem.

PECULIAR MOTION

The universe is getting bigger, it's agreed.
The outer edge expands while within, space
fills, a party balloon of infinite size. The galaxies

move outward, too, their dark centers, the fearsome

black holes, keeping them clustered, bouquets of stars.
Yet astronomers say, a few galaxies move inwards,

fleeing oblivion or whatever lies beyond. "Peculiar motion,"

it's called, when certain arrays—packing mountains, flame,
rocket junk, exhaled breath, planets, oceans, comets, cities

and the mish-mash of all the rest out there—

run for cover. You've got to admire such contrariness.
It's one thing for mortals, shattered by a flick of celestial

funk, to challenge the inevitable. Quite another for the

gassy nebulae to shrug, "No thanks." How would it feel,
I wonder, to traverse the Big Bang's outer shell, time

beneath our boots and—what?—above. Perhaps

that shell is hard as white granite, stepped, little pools of rain
cupped in the hollows. We'd savor the view. And at the top,

after a long and weary climb: a hushed lake, some fish,

a stand of pines. Beneath us, the rainbow of our world,
reminding us of its spectral beauty, pointing us home.

I HAD THIS DREAM

The inner walls of the tent were draped in rugs. Smoke from metal lamps gathered like frayed scarves against the inverted peaks of the roof. There was a low bed and pillows and a table that held an old, heavy book. A man—an Arab chieftain, I thought, though there was no way for me to know this—waited impatiently.

I had no body in the dream, but could read the feelings in the heart of that man and the girl he wanted.

A servant opened the flap that covered the entrance. Another servant led in six girls, covered in veils and long skirts. The man wanted something from them. Of course I assumed it was sex. But then I looked into his heart. I saw that he had no interest in their bodies.

I know this sounds like *The Sheik*, but wait.

The chieftain was young but he knew suffering. He aspired to beauty. He examined the girls, as if by doing so he too could see their hearts. "Do you read?" he asked the first girl. She fell to her knees, shaking her head. "Do you read?" he asked the next. She too said no.

What century was this? What place? It was yesterday, in my head, when I woke in our bed at 3 am.

One girl remained. The servants trembled. The chieftain was furious. He wanted a girl who could read! "Do you read, girl?" he shouted.

She nodded and looked him in the eyes. I saw her heart, at this instant. She could not read. But she wanted to eat.

This is a story I could write for our children. This was my dream.

The chieftain handed her the book. She had never seen anything so frightening, so full of power. She unclasped the jeweled cover. Like an animal, she breathed its scent. Bird scratchings cover the thick skin that was the book's first page. She looked at the man. And she told the first story that came into her head. Since she was hungry, it had to do with food. Since she was a girl, the food was sweet: pastries drenched in honey, sugared nuts, spun sugar in fantastic shapes that pleased a lonely princess.

Sometimes, these stories come to me, in the store or driving in the car.

Of course, the chieftain could not read, either. But he could not tell that this was her story. When she finished, he folded his hands. He looked at her as if she were some witch. But she was still a girl, just a girl, no different from any others he had seen.

"Give her sweets," he said to his servants, "as much as she wants. And she will sleep at my feet."

That is how I left them, the girl eating and the chieftain already impatient for her next story.

What was the book? It was stolen on a raid. It was nothing. It was bird scratchings.

I had this dream.

A THEORY OF STRINGS

If we think of matter as a mix
of light and motion and the whirl
of particles too small to fix

except with probabilities,
well, those are strings, where life begins,
in cows or trees or cowrie shells

washed ashore on Comoros,
tossed on tables, fortune's eyes,
their spotted backs like

river trout, who rising watch
the deep green pools, and leap
and snap at the day's fresh hatch,

star dust, zaps, the minuscule
binding us to the outermost edge
of what we know, the very fuel

of what brings us here, today, right now
our second's breath, the glimpse we have
of the infinite in me and you.

It's a blink, but bottomless,
a radiance in our children's eyes,
that stretches out to nebulas

and the clusters of creation's dust,
at light speed traveling beyond our grasp,
permanent, the sum of us.

CHARLES BRIDGE
for Ray

History. It plods in grey, sooty stone
across the Vltava. Is the river ever not
murky and glum as a Czech? No tourist
points a lens at the banks, the baylets
and verge. They want the statues on the bridge.
Martyrs and knights and boy Jesus. Trapped
with the fogeys! What would he give to skip
like my children from shore to shore? Candy
leaks from pockets. Mittens, too, coins, a glass
dog, pretzel ends, a cheesy wrapper, perhaps
a hotel key. No matter. Things can be found again.
The boy Jesus longs for the swings. He wants
to be dizzy and fall. He craves a fry, jumps
at the plunk of a skipped rock. Would anyone mind
if he dug for treasure? Raced? Kicked a ball
smack into a tour boat? Let's escape, he'd whisper,
just us three. Forget about my granite toes
and old tales and Mom and Dad and the
Vltava's bones. My Father's wrath. What lies
ahead. Comfort rests not in stone, set just so,
but in your cheeks, stung pink by the cold.

MAY DAY

Mother may have cancer
after smoking fifty years.
"Now is not the time," she says,
"for 'I told you sos.'"

My husband's back, freshly stitched,
develops new pain, and he hobbles
like an old man. Too bad the surgeon's
irritating prayers went unheard.

At work, there is cowardice and blame and
just plain fear. I'm fallible. I'm not always
nice. My age spots should belong to
someone older. I never asked for chin hairs.

The galaxy Andromeda moves at a brisk pace
and will one day consume the Milky Way.
I'll be dead then. In other words, I'm mortal.
It galls me to miss such a show.

The cat is senile and pees on the floor.
The dog is senile and pees on the floor.
If I kill them, my daughter will grieve, and I
want her to be twelve and griefless forever.

I wish I was thin and twenty. I wish I had
realized the size of that gift. If I could,
I would take the vampire kiss and diet
on blood and rats and galactical dust.

"How much longer," my son asks,
"till I turn a hundred?" Infinity, I think,
since I will not be there, your cheek will not
be soft and your lips, so perfect, will be as far

as the farthest star from where I sit now,
under the tree, with the sound of cars,
the coffee cold, the day just begun, my fingers
steady as I peck out these words.

BEACON
for Frank Kirk

I flew the pattern at O' Hare,
the city castled and sparkling, air
sucked dry by the cold, the deep,
clenching cold. We're stacked up,
flight after flight. Wing beacons
skim above the lake, shore crusted
in ice floes, and then, darkening,
liquid again and black as tires.

How you'd love this: wind speed,
altitude, the hot roar of the engine
lifting us. Needles whirl as we climb.
Ice cubes in a cup, the rough seat nap:
illusion. To be suspended on skill
and cunning and the flat truth of instrument
flight is danger. "Safe trip," people say.

Nothing about it is safe.
Not the birthing or the living
or the dying. Only death. Who goes
so willingly, in the end?
We can't calculate our escape
as easily as you once plotted flights.
I've seen no maps for this journey.

The pilot says when we'll land.
I imagine it, the touch down, the sudden
contact of the wheels, the sudden heaviness,
the sudden suddenness of it all.
I can almost hear you whisper, "Good,"
as close to prayer as I'll ever come.

ORISON TO THE GODS OF LAKE MICHIGAN

The sun rises; this is what I ask:

For my daughter, tall and sharp-hipped, that she
is not arrested or hit by a drunk driver this,
her senior year. May wise Athena grant less homework,
a lead female role, acceptance letters and financial aid.

For my son, entering that Inferno, middle school,
I entreat steady Kane, tiki god, for wisdom, a thick,
yet still soft skin, humor, sleep, pals, Skittles and
teachers who delight in his bright soul.

For my mother, that Gaia might grant fine journeys
in widowhood, health and a special someone, for
she is not too old. For my stepmother, too, plus
margaritas, parties, concerts and a Roman holiday.

For my lover, I entreat dear Ganesh: entwining
arms that hold and caress and make me gasp.
Patience, too, and the skill of seeming to listen
when I whine. Really sorry about that.

For my sisters, fulfillment. For my brothers, rest.
For the cousins, dead batteries and a Yellow House
under snow and glowing in Bubble Tree light,
Grammy toast and staying up long past bedtime.

For their fathers, may they always be chosen
to get more gas, or the tree, or the fresh bottle
that we drink in Cúchulainn's honor, bold
adventurer, at least in all the old tales.

Buddha, for friends, allow me to be that wise listener
at their best they are for me. For colleagues: a raise
and drinks all around, with salty snacks, Lord.
Coyote: linger elsewhere for a little while, for Earth

grows weary. Tease Mars, pester Jupiter or icy Pluto.
The Abell galaxy is only 13,230 million light-years away.
Concordia, I know you are busy, but make room
for Washington, for we are running out of time.

For me, Ra, sky-master? May my fears be made flesh,
fast as lake runners. May they attach to my skin, a second
skin. May I feel them, dense and hairy, then rinse them
down the cracked drain of my mother's condo.

Gods!

Floating over shells and beer glass, pebbles and bald tires,
sparkling on wavelets that make that barge, pointed north
to Waukegan, look like topaz set in a disk of blue diamonds:
Hear me in your starry chambers! Grant my heart-felt orison!

THE DARK ARMY
for Mark

There is a dark army
of locusts eating me.

Or grasshoppers or spiders,
he says from a hospital bed.

He is paralyzed by a brain
that explodes light showers

behind his eyes. This is a stroke,
but not of luck. This is luck

incarnate, a bearded hitchhiker in
grimy clothes and boots coated

in wet tragedies. Keys found.
Jobs lost. Loves encountered.

And lost. He thumbs his way
into a life and out again,

change and cigarettes in his
pockets, never saying a word.

THANKS TO WHOEVER SAWED THE LIMBS ...

Thanks to whoever sawed the limbs
I dragged curbside, crooked and
splotched as old woman hands.

Pecan and oak, they dropped
in a hurricane, or just because.
When limbs fall, it's like murder,

dumb bombs, fate. Squirrels
chuck with glee, "Wow, yippee,
ha!" Even the cats cower.

The limbs defeated me.

I couldn't cram them into the can.
The heavy trunks cut my palms.
Buy a chain saw, I thought, or

an axe. Such weak weapons against
age, coming for us all. Even trees.
Some day, I'll leave this house

for the quiet hours. The limbs
will fall when I do not hear
and I will not have to bother.

I ATE MY HOUSE

I ate my house
and my 401K, too.
The end comes in dollars and cents
and light and water and the garbage man.
Every month, the groceries.
I ate my house.
The medical bills pile and a lady from Dacca calls
and calls and calls and calls.
The end comes in dollars and cents.
Every month the phone, the heat,
the shot for the cat, the pills for the cat.
I ate my house.
When the roof leaks, I tap
a song to match the dripping drips.
The end comes in dollars and cents.
Every year the pillow flattens.
Wall stains are old friends.
I ate my house.
The end comes in dollars and cents.

WHAT CERES HEARD

Mommy
I need you
Where are you?
Mommy
Scratch my back
I'm hungry
I'm tired
I want
Mommy! I'm scared
Let's go!
Will a tree fall on the house?
Will Grampy die?
Who will be my friend?
Mommy
I don't want to go
I don't want to leave
I don't want to get up or go to sleep
Mom
Mommy, I'm sad
OK
OK
OK
Mom
Whatever
So?
Stop, Mom
Leave me alone
Nothing
No one
Mommy, I'm stupid
Mommy, go away
Mommy! My heart is broken
Mommy. Mommy.
....

Mom.
Mother.
....
I didn't mean to
What are you doing?
I'm going
I'm leaving
I want him
I want.
Did you ever love me?
Can we talk later?
....
Got to go
Listen
He's gone
I'm heart-broken.
I can't talk now
Mommy?
Mom
Mother
...

CARRICK-A-REDE

I want you to hold my hand
until I let go.
By that I mean, when I see the other side

everyone waiting for me
arms open. Happy.
Then I'll release you.

Here's hoping the bridge isn't Carrick-a-Rede
long, narrow and swaying
over the cold North Atlantic.

Bollocks to that, as the Irish say.
I want it to be like a bridge
for sale in Home Depot, a landscape feature.

Mainly the bridge is short.
With a little arch, perhaps.
It's OK if it's made of plastic.

I'll step, holding onto you
from my hospital bed or the chair
like the one that held my Dad

until he released my hand.
Except he'll be waiting for me
on the other side. He'll probably say

"What's with the cheap bridge?
There's a better one on sale at Lowe's
and it's so easy to install."

You'll know when I let go
that I'm safe, I'm arrived
and there's no more cause for sadness.

RED PLANET

I was born on the red planet.
I cultivated the red dust.
I breathed the red sandstorms.
The shared sun rises
with a speed unknown on Earth.

I look at Earth and think:
too blue, too cold, too wet.
I'm red as rocks, red as iron,
red as the blood feeding
my red Martian heart.

I WANT TO KNOW

I want to know the simple things
Like the name of the brown bird on the branch
Or the brown man who picks up the garbage
Every Thursday. I want to know

How is it that a knuckle cracks, or my hair,
the black, wiry one, uninvited, springs
From my chin like a weed after rain.
I pluck it, the hair returns, like an unpaid bill.

Can you explain what's in a tire?
How is it that packaged rice cooks
In perfect grains while real rice sticks
And clumps and packs like clay in the pot?

If I knew these things, I think, the world
Would give me time to contemplate
Mysteries, where life begins,
Where the stars end, where I will go

When none of this matters.

LIKE A WAVE

I tell you I saw it like a wave,
The froth curl, the interior sand
breaking over the bar.

The wave came all the way from Africa.

The globe spins along an orbit
fixed at some specific point,
unknown except we know the point exists.

Oceans heave on its cracked shell.

Then the wave was gone,
pulled back and combined
with the next, rising swell.

I felt alone, but wasn't.

Waves are portents, unruly,
like predators they take,
yet without ever feeling hunger.

I saw it like a wave.

Kirk is the author of *More Terrible Than Death: Massacres, Drugs and America's War in Colombia* and *The Monkey's Paw: New Chronicles from Peru* among other works. An essayist and award-winning poet, she has published widely on issues as diverse as the Andes, family life and pop culture. She holds an MFA in Children's and Young Adult literature from Vermont College of Fine Arts. Kirk teaches human rights at Duke University.

www.ingramcontent.com/pod-product-compliance
Lightning Source LLC
Chambersburg PA
CBHW060224050426
42446CB00013B/3159